"Successful execution of SO required centralized, responsive, and unambiguous C2."

- Joint Pub 3-05 p. III-1

Introduction

The debate surrounding forward-deployed Naval Special Warfare (NSW) Command and Control (C2) has been conducted since before 1987 when Special Operations Forces (SOF) were organized under U.S. Special Operations Command (USSOCOM). Congress mandated the creation of USSOCOM in 1987 to correct serious deficiencies in the ability of the United States to conduct special operations and engage in low-intensity conflict activities.[1]

Why the NSW C2 debate continues today is a mystery considering the unambiguous doctrine and law that were established on the subject. When one examines the variations in theater NSW C2 structures, it becomes clear that there are "doctrine and law offenders" in a chain from the NSW community to the Joint Chiefs of Staff (JCS). Not only is the NSW community itself guilty (at least by not working more aggressively with the U.S. military community to adhere to established doctrine and law), but the JCS, theater Combatant Commanders, Theater Special Operations Commands (TSOC), numbered fleets and component commanders are guilty as well. It is past time to end the debate and restructure NSW C2 in those theaters that violate doctrine and law so that NSW can join its sister SOF components in providing the best possible support to Combatant Commanders worldwide.

This paper outlines the CJCS approved doctrine governing NSW C2, the law that supports it, and brings to light the theater variations in NSW C2 that serve to sustain the debate. It will also identify the issue's possible origin (at least a problem that exists today) that manifests itself in each of the operational theaters, and finally propose clear steps required to bring the offending theaters into compliance. Some theaters NSW C2 structures are more doctrinally mature than others, but all of them require revision in some form.

SOF C2 Doctrine and the Law

The fact that NSW forces are a component of the SOF community is well established and is not currently a subject of debate. As part of the SOF community, it follows that NSW C2 should reflect the same C2 doctrine as the rest of the SOF community. The NSW C2 debate centers on who should have Operational Control (OPCON) of forward deployed NSW forces under "normal circumstances", and who should C2 them during war, operations or contingencies. Each of the theaters outside the continental United States (OCONUS) has a different NSW C2 arrangement.

Doctrinally, JCS publications outline how SOF C2 is to be arranged and without exception, each states SOF C2 should normally be conducted by SOF. "Military doctrine presents fundamental principles that guide the employment of forces. Doctrine is authoritative...though neither policy nor strategy, joint doctrine deals with the fundamental issue of how best to employ the national military power to achieve strategic ends."[2] Therefore, if doctrine is authoritative, why are there variations in who has OPCON of forward deployed NSW forces? As it will become evident, there are variations because the Joint Staff and a host of others ignore prescribed doctrine.

Title 10 of the U.S. Code is very clear who should control SOF in the continental United States (CONUS). "Unless otherwise directed by the Secretary of Defense all active and reserve special operations forces stationed in the United States shall be assigned to the Special Operations Command."[3]

The debate concerns out of the Continental United States (OCONUS) SOF and Title 10 is very clear about SOF deployed OCONUS as well. Title 10 provided for the creation of theater Special Operations Commands (TSOC) which, "As a subunified command of the combatant unified commands is the geographic CINC's[4] source of all expertise in all areas of special operations providing the CINC with a separate element to plan and control the employment of joint SOF in military operations."[5] Stated in plain terms, the TSOCs should have C2 of all OCONUS SOF -- this is the law per Title 10.

Each of the TSOC's roles has been delineated further. "The Theater Special Operations Command, established as a sub-unified command of the combatant unified command is the geographic CINC's source of all expertise in all areas of special operations, providing the CINC with a separate element to plan and control the employment of joint SOF in military operations. The theater SOCs normally exercise Operational Control of SOF (except Civil Affairs and Psychological Operations) within each geographic CINC's area of responsibility."[6]

Without exception, as doctrine provides, the various TSOC commanders have responsibility for SOF assigned to their theaters. "The theater SOC commander is responsible to the geographic CINC for planning and conducting joint special operations in the theater, ensuring that SOF capabilities are matched to mission requirements, exercising operational control of SOF for joint special operations, and advising the CINC and component commanders in theater on the proper employment of SOF."[7]

While SOF's Posture Statement 2000 conveniently articulates its own view of SOF C2 (and therefore NSW C2 as a subset of SOF), it is not doctrine per se, and therefore it could be argued that it is not "authoritative" -- but the Posture Statement 2000 simply restates established and approved joint doctrine.

Joint Pub 3-05 can not be more clear in stating, "Normally, **command and control of SOF should be executed within the SOF chain of command.**"[8] As clear as this guidance seems, joint publications provide additional, multiple references to further reinforce the doctrinal requirement for SOF to exercise C2 of SOF, and the requirements for any commander who may do so.

"Normally C2 of a special operations force is exercised by SOF. Regardless, commanders exercising command authority over SOF should:
- Provide for a clear and unambiguous chain of command;
- Avoid frequent transfer of OPCON of SOF between commanders;
- Provide for sufficient staff experience and expertise to plan, conduct, and support the operations;
- Integrate SOF in the planning process; and
- Match mission capabilities with mission requirements."[9]

This doctrine clearly articulates a commander's requirements to appropriately C2 SOF. The various TSOCs (and designated elements of the TSOC) were *created specifically to meet these requirements* and therefore should C2 and have OPCON of SOF under normal circumstances.[10] "SOF assigned to a theater are under COCOM of the geographic combatant commander. The geographic combatant commander normally exercises COCOM of all assigned and OPCON of all attached SOF through the theater special operations command (SOC)."[11]

Cumulatively then, there can be no doubt that Title 10 and established doctrine, which by definition is authoritative, clearly dictate that SOF C2 (and therefore NSW C2) should be conducted by the TSOC. The TSOC is the *only* OCONUS component that meets the criteria articulated in doctrine to C2 SOF. Simply put, Joint Pub 3-05 is as authoritative as doctrine can be in stating "The theater SOC normally exercises OPCON of all assigned and attached SOF in theater."[12] Because the TSOC is tasked to provide NSW C2, it follows that forward deployed NSW forces should also be OPCON to the TSOC. As clear as doctrine appears to be, there are multiple cases where joint doctrine and Title 10 are violated when it comes to NSW C2.

NSW C2 in the Theaters

Each of the TSOCs has a Naval Special Warfare Unit (NSWU) assigned as a component command except the U.S. European Command (EUCOM) which actually has two NSWUs. The fundamental mission of a NSWU is to provide NSW support to theater operational commanders. Supporting each the the NSWUs is a NSW Squadron (or a NSW Task Unit in one case) which comprises the bulk of forward deployed NSW operational forces.[13]

In all cases, each NSWU is "dual-hatted" meaning it has a formal command relationship with both the TSOC and numbered fleet commander. This dual-hatted structure is a holdover from the time when NSW forces were required to embark and deploy on navy ships as a matter of routine. As a result, NSWUs are called different names. Under the TSOC, it is called a NSWU; under the fleet commander, the NSWU may have a Commander Task Group (CTG) or Commander Task Force (CTF) designation. The various theater C2 arrangements will be discussed in detail later.

One does not need to ponder the notion of a dual-hatted arrangement for long to determine that a NSWU, with two operational chains of command (two "bosses"), clearly does not have a centralized, responsive, and unambiguous C2 arrangement. Graphic illustrations of the NSW C2 relationships in EUCOM and PACOM and SOUTHCOM respectively are provided at Appendices A, B and C to depict how complicated NSW C2 has become.[14] Indeed, most NSWU command relationships are anything but clear, and depending on the situation, forces assigned to a NSWU and its deployed NSW Squadron forces are routinely split, and under the OPCON of two different theater component commanders. Therein lies the C2 problem and source of the NSW C2 debate.

As stated earlier, some theaters have a more mature NSW C2 structure that is slowly evolving closer toward doctrine and law, but for the most part, they all violate them. In order to identify the offenders, one must undertake a study of the various theater NSW C2 arrangements.

NSW C2 in the U.S. European Command (EUCOM)

EUCOM may be the worst doctrine offender of all and will be discussed in detail to illustrate the recurring themes in the other theaters. EUCOM's NSW C2 structure is a disaster with its two geographically separated NSWUs, their resulting separate chains of command, split forces and subsequent diminished unity of effort. Appendix A provides a wire diagram of the NSW C2 arrangement in EUCOM.[15] The diagram illustrates the split in NSW forces between NSWU-2 and NSWU-10 and subsequent split within the NSW Squadron. In the wire diagram, forces OPCON to COMSOCEUR are depicted in purple (i.e. "joint"), and forces OPCON to Commander, U.S. SIXTH Fleet (COMSIXTHFLT) are depicted in blue (i.e. "Navy").

NSWU-2 is geographically situated in Boblingen, Germany just outside Stuttgart (home of SOCEUR), and NSWU-10 is in Rota, Spain. NSWU-2 and its assigned NSW forces are OPCON to COMSOCEUR. NSWU-10 is dual-hatted as NSWU-10 under COMSOCEUR, and CTF 64 under COMSIXTHFLT (homeported in Gaeta, Italy). NSWU-10/CTF 64 is required by EUCOM to split its assigned forces between the two operational commanders. Down to the next level in the chain of command, the deployed NSW Squadron, as a result of having two NSWUs and their two operational commanders, is required to split its forces further in order to accommodate EUCOM's force apportionment under the two operational chains of command.

The confusing result is NSW Squadron forces deployed to the EUCOM NSWUs are fractured; some forces are always under COMSOCEUR OPCON exercised through NSWU-2, some forces are always under COMSOCEUR OPCON exercised under NSWU-10, and some forces are always under COMSIXTHFLT OPCON exercised under CTF 64 (NSWU-10's "fleet hat"). Operationally speaking, neither operational commander "owns" all NSW forces, and therefore can never fully realize NSW's full support. Unity of effort, economy of force and unity of command are all seriously degraded under the EUCOM structure.

Try as the SOCEUR and SIXTHFLT staffs might, shifting forces TACON from one commander to the other never really fixes the problem because there is always the lingering caveat that the commander with OPCON reserves the right to recall its forces to be employed as he sees fit. There have been instances where COMSOCEUR has not employed NSW forces, even though he needed them, simply because they were OPCON to COMSIXTHFLT. Further, because COMSOCEUR does not have OPCON of all NSW forces (and therefore does not have OPCON of all theater SOF -- in violation of doctrine), he can never really even plan to employ the NSW forces that are doctrinally and lawfully his.

COMSOCEUR's roles and responsibilities to CDRUSEUCOM are clear. "As a sub-unified command for special operations, COMSOCEUR provides operational direction and control of special operations, CA and PSYOP forces in the USEUCOM AOR."[16]

With C2 of SOF, COMSOCEUR is responsible for SO throughout the theater and serves as the principle SO advisor to the theater Combatant Commander. "From these varied assets, COMSOCEUR forms task forces capable of executing special operations as well as conducting assessments in response to crisis throughout the USEUCOM AOR."[17] COMSOCEUR also functions as Director, Special Operations Directorate of the EUCOM staff to provide theater strategic input and advice to the commander concerning special operations.[18] Without OPCON of all theater SOF however, COMSOCEUR can not do what he is chartered to do.

USEUCOM is in violation of established doctrine. NSW C2 issues prevent COMSOCEUR from fully exercising his doctrinal responsibilities, and support to theater component commanders, including COMSIXTHFLT, suffers as a result.

NSW C2 in the U.S. Central Command (CENTCOM)

With CENTCOM's and SOF's recent overwhelming successes in Afghanistan and Iraq, one might assume there are no CENTCOM SOF C2 issues. However, an examination of SOF C2 in CENTCOM reveals that the NSW C2 arrangements are by far the most complex, convoluted and least understandable. The CENTCOM NSW C2 structure is so complex that reproducing a wire diagram and attempting to explain it is beyond the scope of this paper.

SOF's posture statement proclaims that Special Operations Command, Central Command (SOCCENT) Forward exercises C2 for all SOF within the AOR.[19] NSWU-3, based in Bahrain, is the NAVSOF component of SOCCENT. Like the EUCOM arrangement, neither SOCCENT nor NSWU-3 exercise OPCON of all the NSW forces in theater. Rather, OPCON of NSW forces are split between the TSOC and fleet commander and NSW force employment is governed by a Memorandum of Understanding (MOU) brokered between U.S. Naval Forces Central Command and SOCCENT.[20]

Not long ago, at least as recently as 1999, the MOU did not exist and NSW forces were under the OPCON of a variety of commands. Deployed fleet Amphibious Ready Groups (ARG) and fleet Carrier Battle Groups (CVBG) had their own embarked NSW Task Unit (NSWTU) composed of a very small NSW C2 element and embarked NSW forces. The NSWTU was OPCON to the ARG or CVBG Task Force Commander, and there was no formal relationship between the deployed fleet NSW forces and the TSOC or NSWU.

The NSW community, led by NSWU-3, successfully argued that basing NSW forces afloat with TF commanders and not under the OPCON of the TSOC was inefficient, violated doctrine and caused lapses in theater NSW presence:

> "The rare occasion for operational flexibility served by having NSW forces embarked aboard ships does not historically, logically or operationally counterbalance the lengthy periods of under-employment and the serious degradation and loss of extremely perishable SOF warfighting skills such as weapons, parachute, demolitions and small unit training. Furthermore because NSW forces embarked aboard ships become tied to ship schedules, the availability of NSW forces in the Persian Gulf under NAVCENT OPCON, is actually far less than eight months per year, leaving significant gaps in fleet NSW SOF forward deployed presence."[21]

Based primarily on the argument that NSW forces under fleet OPCON resulted in presence gaps, NSWU-3 lobbied for OPCON of all deployed NSW forces. While not successful, the debate did result in the MOU which is a step in the right direction.

CENTCOM also violates established doctrine. NSW C2 issues prevent COMSOCCENT from fully exercising his doctrinal responsibilities, and support to theater component commanders, including COMFIFTHFLT, suffers as a result.

NSW C2 in the U.S. Pacific Command (PACOM)

Like all the other theaters, SOF's posture statement claims that Special Operations Command, Pacific (SOCPAC) commands and controls all theater SOF. SOCPAC, located at H.M. Smith, Oahu, Hawaii, is a sub-unified command and serves as the SOF component command for the U.S. Pacific Command.[22] But does SOCPAC have OPCON of all theater SOF? An examination of the NSW C2 arrangement in PACOM reveals clearly they do not. In fact, their C2 arrangement is as convoluted as EUCOM's and is depicted graphically in Appendix B. The biggest difference between EUCOM and PACOM is there is only one NSWU based in Guam that supports the theater so the geographic NSWU split does not exist, but worse, PACOM literally has a triple operational chain of command.[23]

PACOM is not in compliance with prescribed doctrine, and like EUCOM and CENTCOM, NSW forces remain under the OPCON of two operational commanders -- not entirely under the TSOC as doctrine and law prescribe.

NSW C2 in the U.S. Southern Command (SOUTHCOM)

SOUTHCOM's NSW C2 structure is easily the closest to adhering to prescribed doctrine and Title 10. Special Operations Command, South (SOCSO or SOCSOUTH) like the other TSOCs claims is has OPCON of all theater SOF, and it actually does in this case. "SOCSOUTH, is the Southern Command's subordinate unified command for Special Operations. It is responsible for all SOF in the theater except CA and PSYOP forces."[24]

SOUTHCOM's NSW C2 structure is almost ideal -- streamlined, unambiguous and simple -- but there is a nagging, formal relationship with the navy component in SOUTHCOM. Appendix C provides a graphic illustration that clearly shows NSWU-4 and assigned forces under direct SOCSOUTH OPCON with an additional relationship with U.S. Naval Forces South (NAVSO) to support fleet operations when assigned.[25]

The most remarkable difference between SOUTHCOM and the other theaters is that SOUTHCOM does not have a U.S. Navy Fleet Commander and staff resident in theater per se. There is no heavy-handed navy staff to lay claim to the NSW forces or exert undue control. If there was, perhaps SOUTHCOM's C2 relationships would be as doctrinally incorrect and unlawful as the other theaters.

Issues at the Combatant Commander level and Navy Resistance

As described for each of the OCONUS theaters, NSW C2 is generally split between the TSOC and numbered fleet commander. Aside from the obvious that these types of C2 structures do not prescribe to doctrine, there are other tangible and intangible manifestations at the Combatant Commander level.

In a fleet support role, NSW's contribution is often minimized because its forces are split. No single command has OPCON of *all* NSW forces -- so no command can fully employ *all* NSW forces assigned to the theater. The problem remains even if the TSOC is tasked to be a supporting commander to the fleet commander. The fleet and SOC do not realize how well they could support each other in a contingency because the NSWU's forces are split and not available to each commander equally. Additionally in EUCOM, NSWU-2 has no direct support role to the fleet under SOCEUR as its sole master so EUCOM suffers from a double NSW chain of command.

TSOCs are reluctant to commit forces to fleet supported contingency because they may not be available when the TSOC needs to respond to a crisis. Conversely, the fleet commanders are not willing to commit allocated forces to the TSOC for the same reason. As a result, the theater NSWU responsible to the fleet commander under some arrangement, can not solicit additional SOF options in support of fleet contingencies from the TSOC because under the current C2 structures, the TSOCs have no formal tasking to provide support based on individual NSWU fleet-imposed requirements.

Perhaps insight into the Navy's history with SOF and Navy culture can shed some light on why the issue prevails. The Navy vigorously resisted NSW's assignment to USSOCOM from the very beginning (prior to 1987), and it took a contentious ruling by then Secretary of Defense Casper Weinberger to get the Navy aboard. So strong were the Navy's feelings that even after Secretary Weinberger left office, the Navy attempted to get his decision reversed!

> "...the Navy, for example, is doing everything they can now to avoid being put into this program [USSOCOM]. I mean, the Navy SEALs--the Secretary of the Navy--I believe it is the Secretary of the Navy--objected to SEALs being included in SOF and after Weinberger left, we get the new secretary and they appeal to him to override Secretary Weinberger's decision which further underscores the difficulty we have in putting SOF together..."[26]

Fortunately, USSOCOM prevailed in the argument. General Lindsay (then USSOCOM Commander) argued that NSW forces belonged to USSOCOM because they were based in the United States, and NSW's relationship to the fleets was no different than a Special Forces Group's assignment to a particular theater, and he wanted to integrate NSW with other SOF.[27] That very logic still applies today -- NSW's relationship with the Navy is no different than Army Special Force's is to the Army, or Air Force Special Operations force's to the Air Force -- and they aren't having C2 debates. But the Navy continues to resist.

The Navy as an institution resists change and has an inbred "need to control" that it must be willing to relinquish if it is to fully realize the benefits NSW and the SOF communities can provide. The Navy's reputation of being less likely to work well in a truly joint environment, its propensity to "go it alone", stems from the C2 issue, manifests itself in misuse, under-utilization, and SOF/NSW under-representation in campaigns, operations and contingencies. If the Navy truly wants to be "joint", changing NSW C2 is an opportunity to prove it and reap its rewards.

Where does the NSW C2 problem begin?

OCONUS NSW C2 is destined to be doctrinally incorrect and in violation of Title 10 even before forces deploy. The Joint Staff, either due to mistrust in the theater Combatant Commander's ability to allocate NSW forces in theater, misunderstanding of doctrine, or disregard for doctrine and Title 10 are the first on the list of "doctrine and law offenders." While the Joint Staff has the authority to provide specific direction for Combatant Commanders, it is contrary to the doctrine they write and publish. Ironically, the very staff that is chartered to prescribe doctrine violates it.

A Combatant Commander has the responsibility for "organizing and employing commands and forces".[28] Additionally, Combatant Commanders have the responsibility to "prescribe the chain of command within their commands and designate the appropriate level of command authority to be exercised by subordinate commanders."[29]

NSW forces are assigned to a Combatant Commander's Area of Responsibility (AOR) via a JCS Deployment Order (DEPORD), and the Combatant Commander is responsible for organizing and assigning those forces to meet theater requirements. However, recent JCS DEPORDS have usurped this responsibility by designating where and in what quantity those NSW forces allocated to a specific theater should be assigned. While not specifically directing it, but implying it through direction on where and in what quantity to locate the NSW forces in theater, the DEPORD actually implies who should have OPCON of the deployed force.[30]

For example, in a JCS DEPORD for NSW forces deploying to EUCOM, NSW forces were directed to be divided between U.S. Naval Forces Europe (OPCON to NAVEUR and positioned in Rota, Spain) and SOCEUR (OPCON to COMSOCEUR and positioned in Stuttgart, Germany).[31] This usurps the Combatant Commander's authority, and is the genesis for NSW forces not being properly assigned under TSOC OPCON. Interestingly, no Combatant Commander has challenged the Joint Staff's methods.

The Correct NSW C2 Structure and Justification

Unfortunately, all OCONUS theaters violate SOF C2 doctrine so there is no good example in practice to illustrate how NSW C2 should be structured. Based on doctrine and Title 10, a basic, unambiguous structure can be easily created and it would most closely resemble SOUTHCOM's. Under the doctrinally and lawfully correct structure, all forward deployed NSW forces would be under TSOC OPCON. By virtue of their

component status, each component can identify requirements to the SOF component to

satisfy. To illustrate, a generic wire diagram is provided at Figure 1.

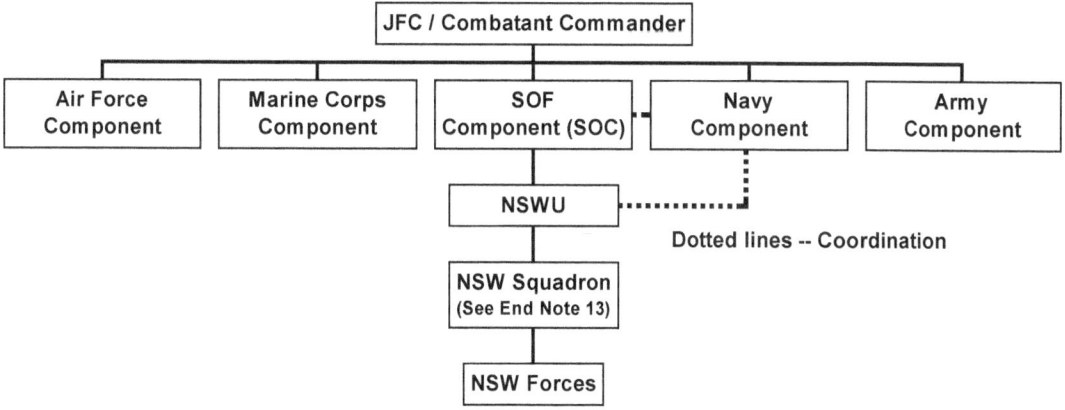

Figure 1 - Generic NSW C2 structure

This simple NSW C2 structure meets the Joint Pub 3-05 doctrinally established

criteria for commanding and controlling SOF and has several inherent advantages:

- It provides a clear and unambiguous chain of command under normal circumstances. It is streamlined, provides the TSOC Commander flexibility, provides unity of command and unity of effort.
- It avoids OPCON transfers between commanders. Adhering to the "requirements based tasking" and prioritization methods, the TSOC can match requirements with the best possible tailored SOF package.
- The TSOC staff experience and expertise to plan, rehearse, conduct and support operations are always available. The TSOC Commander can execute his duties as the Combatant Commander's SOF advisor. The TSOC staff can provide the tailored, operational and tactical level intelligence SOF requires. The TSOC can maintain the authority to deploy and re-deploy SOF support, plus employ its organic mobility options in support.
- The TSOC can allocate appropriate SOF to integrate into the planning process, and provide trained liaison personnel where needed.
- It provides a means for the Navy Component to coordinate SOF activities with the TSOC and theater NSWU.

This simple arrangement provides the JFC a "one stop shop" for SOF support. All the JFC has to do during the planning process is use the assigned SOF JFC liaison personnel to identify SOF mission requirements for the TSOC to support.

Each of the OCONUS numbered fleet staffs has a NSW Officer assigned. The fleet staff NSW Officer should be re-designated as a "SOF Liaison Officer". His job should be to coordinate SOF support between the fleet, TSOC and NSWU. Ultimately, the theater Combatant Commander would receive the best possible SOF support tailored to mission requirements.

Arguments Against Change

There are strenuous arguments against changing the NSW C2 structure including lingering concerns over change proposals that will "drive a wedge between NSW and the fleet." The Navy's resistance to "giving up" NSW to USSOCOM were outlined earlier. If calmly and unemotionally reasoned however, most arguments against changing NSW C2 to conform to doctrine can be put to rest.

There are definitely instances when Tactical Control of NSW forces should be transferred to one theater component or another to support operational requirements, but they should always remain within a SOF C2 structure. The Navy must grow out of its "need to control" culture if it ever is to realize the full benefits of SOF support. Embarking NSW or SOF in Navy shipping "just in case" they are needed (and are therefore close at hand) has been the historic -- albeit invalid -- argument.

> "Possession of NSW forces for the sole purpose of ownership to "enhance" [the] Fleet Commander's "Tool Kit" [which] is what happens frequently to NSW. A Fleet Commander is unwilling to give up OPCON of NSW due to lack of understanding [of] the OPCON/TACON relationships or his simple unwillingness to give "Anything" he owns to another force not in his chain of command."[32]

Split OPCON proponents believe the current system works and there is no need to change it. They argue that if the fleet commander has to go to the TSOC for support, a "Request for Forces bureaucratic layer" has been added. This is not true, especially if the TSOC is designated as a supporting commander to the JFC -- as it should be -- and the assigned SOF liaison personnel do their job. The JFC simply has to identify a SOF requirement and the TSOC (as JFSOCC or JSOTF) fills the requirement with a tailored SOF package.

Under a different scenario, what if the TSOC argues he needs all NSW forces during a contingency or operation and the fleet commander declares he needs NSW support but no additional NSW forces are available? Arguably this is a realistic possibility, but it has never happened. A reality of today's operational world is that there are more requirements for NSW support than there are NSW forces, and this is not going to change. Each of the theater Combatant Commanders has to prioritize resources against requirements -- this is why there are four star Combatant Commanders in each theater -- to prioritize and task subordinate commanders. It is the Combatant Commander's responsibility to prioritize to determine which subordinate commander receives NSW support when there aren't sufficient forces to meet requirements.

Most OCONUS theaters have established Memorandums of Agreement (MOA) governing NSW support between the TSOC and Navy components. While a MOA between the fleet and SOC may avert the fleet commander's concerns over "not having NSW forces when he needs them", it should not direct a quantity or force size that will be made available to him "under normal circumstances". Rather, it should pledge support consistent with other requirements for routine activities such as exercises and engagement activities that are consistent with instances when SOF support would be provided in war, operations or contingencies. A properly negotiated MOA has utility, but routine or recurring activities conducted in support of the fleet should be done so within the SOF chain of command.

Steps to Correct the Discrepancies

As outlined earlier, the beginning of the NSW C2 problem begins even before forces deploy under a JCS DEPORD. The first step in ending the NSW C2 problem is for the Joint Staff to get out of the business of directing the Combatant Commanders where to allocate their forces and to whom to assign OPCON when promulgating the NSW DEPORD. Allocating and assigning forces within a theater is the Combatant Commander's job to do.

The second step is for Combatant Commanders, in accordance with doctrine and law, to assign OPCON of forward deployed NSW forces to the TSOC under the NSW C2 structure that was described earlier. The Combatant Commander must allow the TSOC Commander to execute his duties and responsibilities that are articulated in joint doctrine.

Step three, upon accepting OPCON of forward deployed NSW forces, the TSOC should delegate and exercise OPCON through a single theater NSWU. Each NSWU was established to support and C2 NSW in theater, and is the best TSOC component entity to do so. As the focal point for all special operations in their respective theaters, TSOCs should take an immediate and aggressive role to correct this discrepancy. It is in the theater's best interest.

Fourth, the OCONUS numbered fleet commanders should re-designate their staff NSW Operations Officer to "SOF Liaison Officer" and task him to: 1) Assist his staff in identifying appropriate SOF support; 2) Request additional SOF liaison personnel during crisis planning; and 3) Coordinate SOF requirements with the TSOC and NSWU (if applicable). Essentially, the fleet staff "SOF Liaison Officer" should function as the bridge between the fleet staff and TSOC to coordinate appropriate SOF support.

Finally, Combatant Commanders should task their respective SOC and Navy components to draft a simple, sensible, supportable and enduring MOA to ensure support for routine theater NSW requirements.

Conclusion

Any notion that NSW forces are forward deployed solely to support naval missions, and therefore should be in a C2 arrangement that facilitates support only to naval missions as a matter of routine operations, is in violation of the Congressional mandate that created USSOCOM in 1987. Unfortunately, this notion is what current NSW C2 architectures accomplish. While Navy by service, *NSW forces are not naval forces -- they are, by law and doctrine joint SOF assets* -- and should be commanded and controlled as such. The Joint Staff, EUCOM, PACOM, CENTCOM and SOUTHCOM are all in violation of joint doctrine and Title 10.

SOF and their respective C2 structures have been an issue since before USSOCOM's creation. The Army and Air Force have reconciled their C2 evolution, but the Navy maintains its outdated and doctrinally incorrect C2 structure with respect to NSW.

It is time for the Navy to let go of tradition and "the old way of doing business" and relinquish NSW OPCON to the TSOCs. It is time for the Combatant Commanders to establish the correct NSW C2 structure within their theaters in accordance with their responsibilities. It is time for each TSOC to demand NSW OPCON so they can execute their duties in support of their commanders. Finally, it is time for the NSW community to stand up and take aggressive steps to push the required changes and stop hallucinating about driving a wedge between the NSW community and its parent service.

The recommended C2 structure provided is an example for all theaters to adopt if they truly desire to receive the best possible NSW (and SOF) support, and ultimately win at war or succeed during operations short of war.

END NOTES

[1] Office of the Assistant Secretary of Defense (Special Operations/Low Intensity Conflict), <u>United States Special Operations Forces Posture Statement 2000</u> (Washington, DC: 2000), 11.

[2] Joint Chiefs of Staff, <u>Joint Warfare of the Armed Forces of the United States</u>, Joint Pub 1 (Washington DC: 10 January 1995), vi.

[3] General Military Law, <u>U.S. Code, Title 10</u>, sec. 167 (1992)

[4] For purposes of this paper "geographic CINC" or "CINC" have been updated to mean "Combatant Commanders" in today's terminology in accordance with SECDEF's direction in January 2002.

[5] General Military Law, <u>U.S. Code, Title 10</u>, sec. 167 (1992)

[6] Office of the Assistant Secretary of Defense (Special Operations/Low Intensity Conflict), <u>United States Special Operations Forces Posture Statement 2000</u> (Washington, DC: 2000), 13.

[7] Ibid.

[8] Joint Chiefs of Staff, <u>Doctrine for Joint Special Operations</u>, Joint Pub 3-05 (Washington DC: 17 April 1998), ix.

[9] Ibid., III-1.

[10] Elements of the various TSOCs that are meet the C2 requirements stipulated in this doctrine are labeled with different designations. Under normal circumstances, such as an operation or contingency, the Joint Special Operations Task Force (JSOTF) or a derivative of a JSOTF is the appropriate C2 organization. Under a Joint Task Force scenario, the Joint Force Special Operations Component Commander (JFSOCC) would be the appropriate CJTF supporting commander to C2 SOF.

[11] Joint Chiefs of Staff, <u>Doctrine for Joint Special Operations</u>, Joint Pub 3-05 (Washington DC: 17 April 1998), III-2.

[12] Ibid.

[13] In order to understand a theater-by-theater analysis of NSW C2, one needs to understand how NSW forces are currently structured during forward deployments. In April 2003, NSW began deploying under a new concept called "Naval Special Warfare 21" (NSW 21). Based on a composite squadron concept, similar to a Carrier Battle

Group Air Wing or Destroyer Squadron, a standard SEAL Team is augmented by detachments from a Special Boat Team, SEAL Delivery Vehicle Team and other support elements 180 days prior to deployment. This composite group, led by a SEAL O-5 Commanding Officer, is redesignated as a "NSW Squadron" and spends its last 180 days conducting integration training so they are a single, unified, effective and interoperable force when they deploy OCONUS. The NSW Squadron CO reports directly to the NSWU CO. In theory, the NSWU CO identifies support requirements to the NSW Squadron CO who task organizes his composite forces to meet requirements.

[14] Kidd, Gregory R. <kiddg@nswu10.nswlant.socom.smil.mil> and Volk, Christopher. <volkc@nswu1.socom.smil.mil> "Request for Information." [E-mails to John Houfek <houfekj@nwc.navy.smil.mil> 17 April 2003. Graphics reproduced to remain unclassified.

[15] Kidd, Gregory R. <kiddg@nswu10.nswlant.socom.smil.mil> "Request for Information." [E-mail to John Houfek <houfekj@nwc.navy.smil.mil> 17 April 2003. Graphic reproduced to remain unclassified.

[16] Office of the Assistant Secretary of Defense (Special Operations/Low Intensity Conflict), United States Special Operations Forces Posture Statement 2000 (Washington, DC: 2000), 21.

[17] Ibid.

[18] Ibid.

[19] Office of the Assistant Secretary of Defense (Special Operations/Low Intensity Conflict), United States Special Operations Forces Posture Statement 2000 (Washington, DC: 2000), 24.

[20] Tankersley, Stephen A. <tankersley@nswu3.bahrain.navy.smil.mil> "Request for Information." [E-mail to John Houfek <houfekj@nwc.navy.smil.mil> 17 April 2003.

[21] Elliot, Stewart G. Operational Control of Forward Deployed Naval Special Warfare Forces. Naval War College. Newport, RI: 18 May 2001. 13.

[22] Office of the Assistant Secretary of Defense (Special Operations/Low Intensity Conflict), United States Special Operations Forces Posture Statement 2000 (Washington, DC: 2000), 27.

[23] Volk, Christopher. <volkc@nswu1.socom.smil.mil> "Request for Information." [E-mail to John Houfek <houfekj@nwc.navy.smil.mil> 17 April 2003. Graphic reproduced to remain unclassified.

[24] Office of the Assistant Secretary of Defense (Special Operations/Low Intensity Conflict), United States Special Operations Forces Posture Statement 2000 (Washington, DC: 2000), 18.

[25] Kilrain, Colin. <kilrainc@nswu4.socom.smil.mil> "Request for Information." [E-mail to John Houfek <houfekj@nwc.navy.smil.mil> 23 April 2003.

[26] Kasich, John R. Statement before the Special Operations Panel Subcommittee on Readiness Committee on Armed Services 23 February 1988. U.S. Government Printing Office, Washington, D.C. H.A.S.C. No. 100-58. 46.

[27] United States Special Operations Command, United States Special Operations Command History (MacDill Air Force Base, FL: September, 1998), 12.

[28] Joint Chiefs of Staff, Doctrine for Joint Operations, Joint Pub 3-0 (Washington, DC: 01 February 1995), 6.

[29] Joint Forces Staff College, Joint Staff Officer's Guide, Pub 1, 2000, 1-29 and 1-31.

[30] Joint Chiefs of Staff, CJCS Deployment Order for NSW Forces, (Washington, DC: 23 July 2002).

[31] Ibid.

[32] Ehret, Jason, quoted in Stewart G. Elliot, Operational Control of Forward Deployed Naval Special Warfare Forces. Naval War College. Newport, RI: 18 May 2001. 8.

BIBLIOGRAPHY

Collins, James W. Blue and Purple: Optimizing the Command and Control of Forward Deployed Naval Special Warfare. U.S. Army Command and General Staff College. Fort Leavenworth, KS: 1997

Commander, U.S. Naval Forces Europe/Commander, Special Operations Command Europe Memorandum of Agreement. June 1998.

Davis, Harley C. Special Operations Forces: Prospectives of Employment and Command and Control in Peace and War. National War College, National Defense University. Washington, D.C.: March 1985.

Elliot, Stewart G. Operational Control of Forward Deployed Naval Special Warfare Forces. Naval War College. Newport, RI: 18 May 2001.

General Military Law. U.S. Code, Title 10, sec. 167 (1992).

General Accounting Office. Special Operations Forces Opportunities to Preclude Overuse and Misuse. Report to the Chairman, Subcommittee on Military Readiness, Committee on National Security, House of Representatives. Washington, DC: May 1997.

Harris, Scott A. Command, Control and Integration of Special Operations Forces into the General Purpose Force. Naval War College. Newport, RI: 08 February 2000.

Hughes, Wayne P. The Power in Doctrine. Naval War College Review. Summer 1995.

Joint Chiefs of Staff. CJCS Deployment Order for NSW Forces. Washington, D.C.: 23 July 2002.

Joint Chiefs of Staff. Doctrine for Command, Control, Communications and Computer (C4) Systems Support to Joint Operations. Joint Pub 6-0. Washington, D.C.: 30 May 1995.

Joint Chiefs of Staff. Doctrine for Joint Operations. Joint Pub 3-0. Washington, D.C.: 01 February 1995.

Joint Chiefs of Staff. Doctrine for Joint Special Operations. Joint Pub 3-05. Washington, D.C.: 17 April 1998.

Joint Chiefs of Staff. Joint Special Operations Operational Procedures. Joint Pub 3-05.3. Washington, D.C.: 25 August 1993.

Joint Chiefs of Staff. Joint Warfare of the Armed Forces of the United States. Joint Pub 1.
    Washington D.C.: 10 January 1995.

Joint Forces Staff College. Joint Staff Officer's Guide. Pub 1. 2000.

Kidd, Gregory R. <kiddg@nswu10.nswlant.socom.smil.mil> "Request for Information."
    [E-mail to John Houfek <houfekj@nwc.navy.smil.mil> 17 April 2003.

Kilrain, Colin. <kilrainc@nswu4.socom.smil.mil> "Request for Information." [E-
    mail to John Houfek <houfekj@nwc.navy.smil.mil> 23 April 2003.

Locher, James R., III. Victory on the Potomac. Texas A&M University Press. College
    Station, TX: 2002.

Office of the Assistant Secretary of Defense (Special Operations/Low Intensity Conflict).
    United States Special Operations Forces Posture Statement 2000. Washington, D.C.:
    2000

Tankersley, Stephen A. <tankersley@nswu3.bahrain.navy.smil.mil> "Request for
    Information." [E-mail to John Houfek <houfekj@nwc.navy.smil.mil> 17 April 2003.

United States Special Operations Command. United States Special Operations Command
    History. MacDill Air Force Base, FL: September 1998.

United States Government Printing Office. Statement before the Special Operations Panel
    Subcommittee on Readiness Committee on Armed Services. House Armed Services
    Committee No. 100-58. Washington, D.C: 23 February 1988.

Volk, Christopher. <volkc@nswu1.socom.smil.mil> "Request for Information." [E-mail
    to John Houfek <houfekj@nwc.navy.smil.mil> 17 April 2003.

EUCOM - NSW C2 Structure

Appendix A

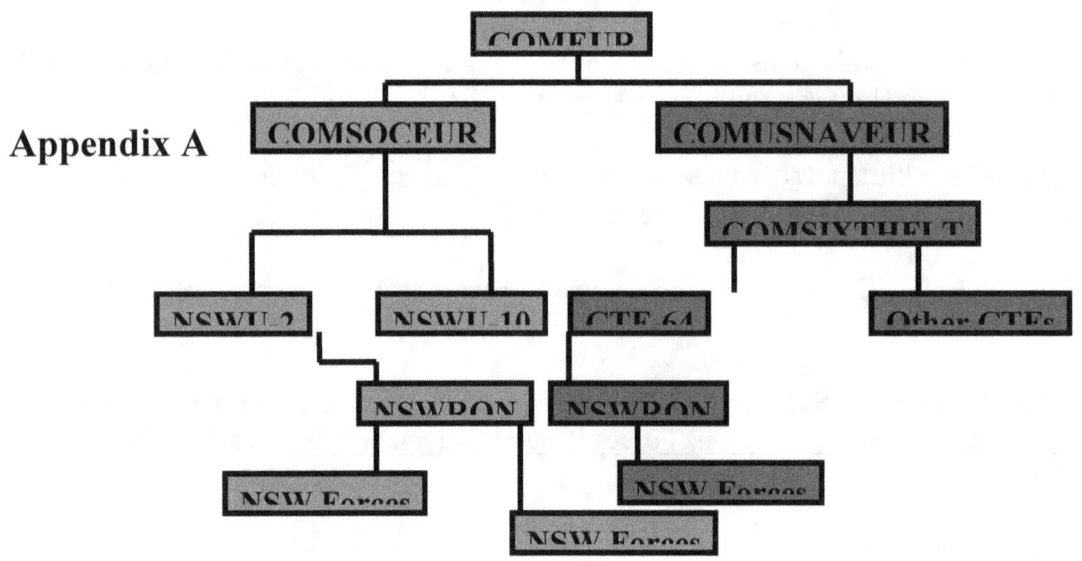

Note: Forces in purple are OPCON to COMSOCEUR; forces in blue are OPCON to COMSIXTHFLT

PACOM - NSW C2 Structure

Appendix B

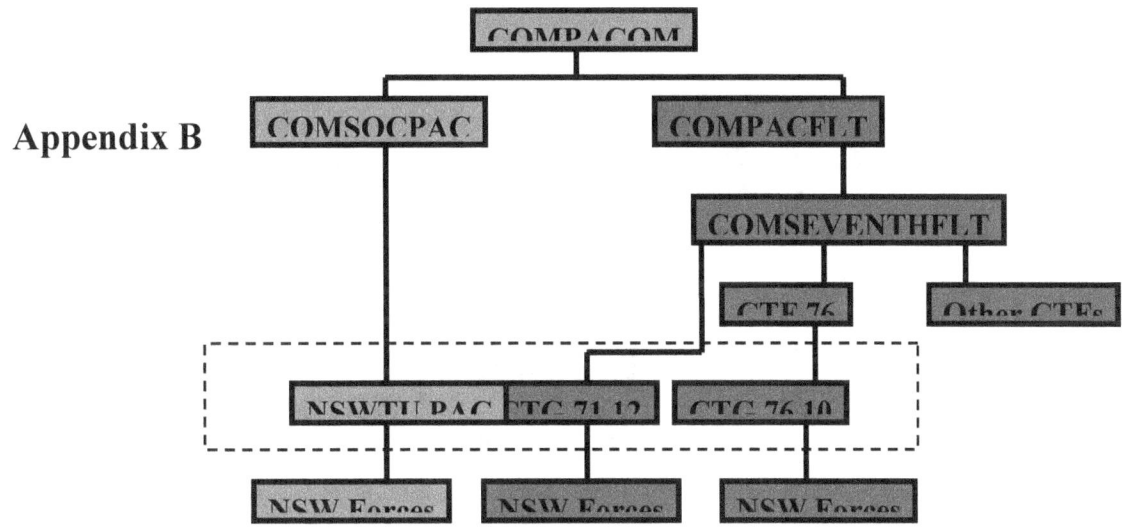

Notes: Forces in purple are OPCON to COMSOCPAC; forces in blue are OPCON to

COMSEVENTHFLT. NSWU-1 wears all three hats depicted in dashed box.

SOUTHCOM - NSW C2 Structure

Appendix C

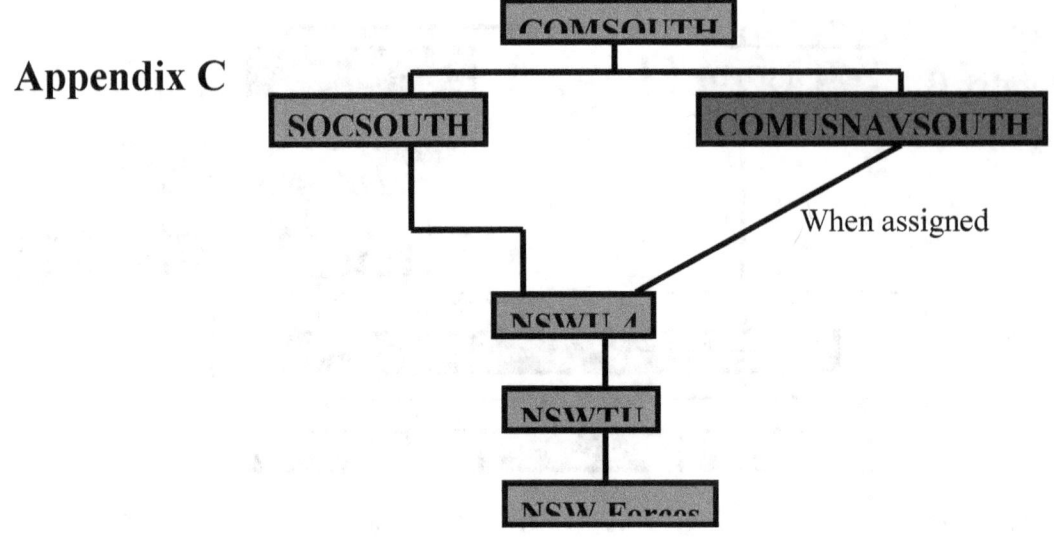

www.ingramcontent.com/pod-product-compliance
Lightning Source LLC
Chambersburg PA
CBHW080801290526
45790CB00008B/3540